THE LOST VILLAGES
OF SUSSEX

THE LOST VILLAGES
OF SUSSEX

JOHN E. VIGAR

THE DOVECOTE PRESS

First published in 1994 by The Dovecote Press Ltd
Stanbridge, Wimborne, Dorset BH21 4JD

ISBN 1 874336 29 6

Photoset in Palatino by The Typesetting Bureau
Wimborne, Dorset
Printed and bound by Biddles Ltd
Guildford and Kings Lynn

Contents

The main MAP is on pages 6/7.
The 16 page plate section falls between pages 64/65.

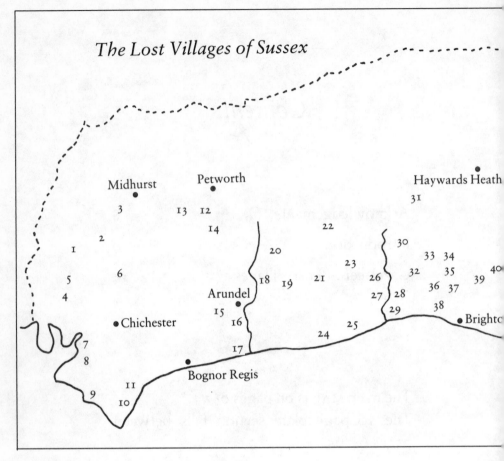

The Lost Villages of Sussex

Midhurst
3

Petworth
13   12
14

Haywards Heath
31

2
1

20

22

30

33 34

5   6

18 19

21

23

26

32

35
36 37

40

39

4

Arundel
15

16

Chichester

17

Bognor Regis

7
8
9   11
10

24   25

27   28
29   38

Brighton

Location of villages mentioned in main text

1.	The Mardens	17.	Islesham (Climping)
2.	Chilgrove	18.	Burpham
3.	Linch	19.	Upper Barpham
4.	Racton	20.	Parham
5.	Lordington	21.	Muntham
6.	Binderton	22.	Warminghurst
7.	Apuldram	23.	Wiston
8.	East Itchenor	24.	West Tarring
9.	Bracklesham	25.	Heene
10.	Old Selsey	26.	Botolphs
11.	Wardour (Sidlesham)	27.	Coombes
12.	Burton	28.	Old Erringham
13.	Duncton	29.	Shoreham, Old and New
14.	Glatting	30.	Woodmancote
15.	Binsted	31.	Twineham
16.	Ford	32.	Perching

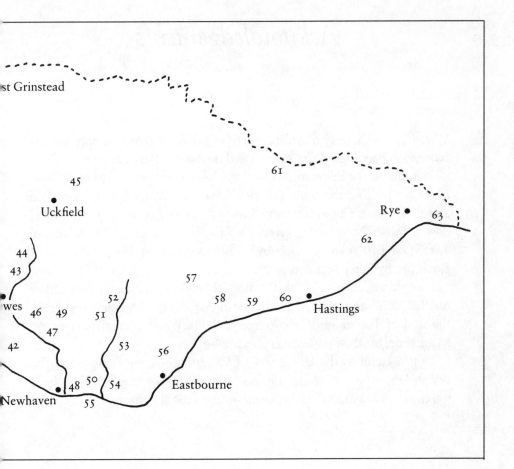

Acknowledgements

Whilst researching and writing this book I have relied heavily on the Sussex Archaeological Collections and the Sussex Records Society.

In addition the following works have been consulted: *The Lost Villages of Britain* by Richard Muir, *Deserted Medieval Villages* by M. Beresford and J. G. Hurst, *Domesday Book*: Sussex, *Victoria History of the County of Sussex, Sussex Notes and Queries, The History of Sussex* by M. A. Lower, *The South East from AD 1000* by P. Brandon and B. Short, *The Sussex Landscape* by Peter Brandon.

I would also like to thank the staff of the East Sussex Record Office for their kind attention to my requests for information, and especially the staff of Tunbridge Wells Reference Library and Springfield Library, Maidstone, for their patience and expertise.

I am grateful to the University of Cambridge Aerial Survey and the British Library for allowing the use of illustrations for which they hold the copyright, and to Angela Ewing for drawing the maps.

Introduction

The history of England is one of moving populations. Well-known conquests by the Romans, Saxons, Normans, and smaller groups such as the Hugenots, have all made England what it is today. The influences which have emanated from these various people have all had an effect on the look and feel of the regions in which we live. As one of the southernmost coastal counties in England, Sussex has probably been influenced more than most areas – with more people arriving and settling than just passing through.

As an historian I feel that our appreciation of topographical and architectural history is often biased towards continual progress and improvement. Yet so often in our history there has also been marked regression and failure – features that are rarely studied as they are not as easy to represent.

Until the short lived Iron boom of the seventeenth century, and the slightly later growth of seaside resorts, Sussex was predominantly an agricultural county, the majority of settlements having their origins in the well-established techniques of farming in either arable or animal husbandry. It follows, therefore, that the first settlers chose locations that suited their agrarian requirements.

It should be stated from the outset that references to a particular place do not necessarily refer to a set location for a village, but only to an area of land within defined boundaries. It is more than likely that until the tenth century – and in certain instances long after – populations were mobile within their boundaries, settling in any one area as long as climatic, financial or social influences allowed. This book will try to identify some of the earlier sites for surviving settlements, as well as those places which have completely disappeared.

There are, inevitably, perhaps a dozen or so sites in the county – Berwick and Ore remain two of the most elusive in terms of documentation – that are generallly accepted as being depopulated. Sadly, there is at present scant evidence as to the size of these original settlements, and

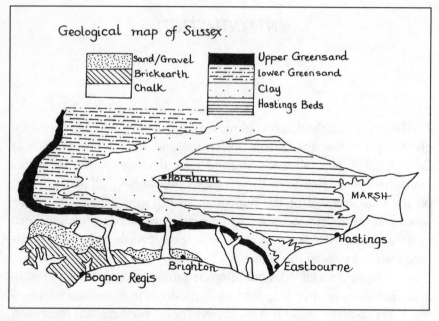

By comparing this map to the one on pages 6 and 7 it will be seen that there is a definite pattern to the distribution of deserted villages, the majority being on the lighter soils to the south of the Upper Greensand ridge.

the reasons which led to them becoming 'lost'.

A glance at the map of Sussex will show that the majority of 'lost' villages that we do know something about are to be found in the southern coastal strip. Here the geology was directly responsible for the original settlement, the later movement of the village within its manorial boundary, and the eventual abandonment of the site completely.

The agricultural practices of the medieval period are today much better understood than they were. We no longer regard them as being simplistic black and white categories of arable and animal husbandry. Indeed, there is evidence in Sussex, where early ecclesiastical records survive, that a very complicated system of mixed farming was used from the eighth century onwards.

It would be fair to say that all early settlements were predominantly arable establishments, with the type of crop grown dependant upon the exact geology of the area. The very light soils on the exposed tops of the South Downs were suitable for oats and rye; the middle slopes —

protected from the severe coastal winds – could be used for barley; with the lower valley floors with their heavy clays being suitable only for dredge, a mixture of barley and oats. The latter was often grown in conjunction with legumes – to add nitrogen to the soil in a systematic rotation. This was not as successful on the very tops of the Downs, and it is here that sheep (and other animal husbandry) makes an appearance.

By keeping sheep in downland folds it was possible to add nitrogen and body to the light soils. In addition the sheep provided fleeces for sale, and meat for local consumption. As the price of wool steadily climbed, so more and more flocks were introduced, gradually becoming the predominant form of agriculture. Less people were required to tend the flocks, and as arable farming declined, so a marked number of people moved from the isolated downland settlements to the prosperous ports and towns. However, the majority of fleeces produced in the south of England during the twelfth and thirteenth centuries were exported to Italy via France, and export duties introduced by Edward I in the 1290s to raise funds for military campaigns started to hit the demand for English fleeces, and wool gradually became less viable as a main product. Later wars with France effectively put a complete dampener on wool exports for a number of years, and it wasn't until the English cloth trade had developed that the production of wool was once again the most advantageous form of agriculture in which to be.

Without the benefit of hindsight, it seemed that in the last half of the thirteenth century wool production was the correct form of agriculture, and people moved away from the country in large numbers. This left many settlements with their lowest population levels since their foundation. Then in the summer of 1349 the Black Death hit this skeleton population very badly indeed, with the result that those communities that really were struggling to get their finances in the black were forced to give up the fight. Even those villages that were able to continue had insufficient workers to reintroduce the now much-needed cereal crops essential for the maintenance of a stable population nationwide.

This is the main point to be brought out by this book – that the much quoted desertion of villages due to the Black Death should be seen in a wider context, as in almost all cases these villages had started to decline fifty years before the arrival of the plague. That the plague compounded the problems is not an issue of contention – the acceptance that there were problems beforehand is the key to understanding the more complex nature of this issue.

In many instances the change from arable to sheep farming was just a case of putting animals on the same land. However, such was the profit to be made in those early heady years that enormous efforts were made to create the optimum conditions for sheep husbandry. This was particularly true of the manors owned by monastic foundations – in Sussex those of Lewes and Battle being to the forefront of these changes. Both landlords reclaimed large areas of former saltmarsh along the south coast to provide fertile grazing lands, although time quickly showed these investments to have been improvident.

None of our sources of documentary evidence are entirely reliable, making it extremely difficult to work out population size during the medieval period. With the exception of a few manorial rolls that give fairly accurate information for a given moment in time, there are no comprehensive records to be found. Therefore, we are forced to look at the national records that were compiled to cover the whole of our area in the hope that by comparing a number of entries we are able to discover some general patterns that will lead us to discover 'lost' villages.

The earliest comprehensive survey available to us is the Domesday Book of 1086. This by no means deserves the reputation it has gained over the centuries. It is inaccurate, vague and wildly inconsistent. However, it is the first wide scale source available to us and must be used as a first step towards population study. Like all the later surveys we have at our disposal, the population figures in the Domesday Survey are much lower than they were in reality, counting the heads of households rather than actual people. For this reason modern commentators suggest multiplying the Domesday figures by up to five to get a more realistic population.

Frequently in the Domesday entries there are references to two types of manorial resident. The villein was basically a tied tenant who could farm the land he had been granted by the lord of the manor. In return he was expected to provide labour at the lord's bidding. This often involved a large proportion of his work. The slave held no land from the lord, and worked as his absolute servant. The presence of a slave frequently implies that the lord of the manor was a resident rather than absentee landlord. The slave had been a common feature of the Saxon manorial system, but was virtually unknown in the Norman tradition, and over a period of forty or fifty years this class of citizen was absorbed into the ever-growing villeinage.

Similarly, the amount of land recorded in the Survey varies considerably. It is usually given in the form of hides and virgates. The hide in Saxon England was the amount of land that could support one family, but by the time of Domesday it probably equated to about 120 acres, with a virgate forming a quarter of a hide. As we look at the population figures and compare them to the number of hides in the same entry we find that the amount of land often fails to tie in with the size of population. This only goes to remind us that the Survey was an assessment of the value of the land rather than its actual size.

Later documents are equally unreliable. For the late thirteenth and early fourteenth centuries we have lists of taxable residents of each parish. Where all four returns (1296, 1327, 1332 and 1334) survive for each parish we can at least get an idea as to whether the population was rising or falling, but beyond that they can be of little help. For instance the figures again refer to the heads of households – and only those households where the head was sufficiently well off to be taxed. The numbers of people exempt from tax were not recorded. If we again use our Domesday multiplication this brings us to a minimum, rather than actual, population size.

In the seventeenth century two surveys of religious conformity were compiled – which between them help fill a noticeable gap in documentary sources – but again these figures can not be subjected to close scrutiny on an individual parochial basis. Also of that period are the Hearth Tax returns which record the larger houses that had hearths. Unless we have other sources of information as to where these houses were in relation to a main community they can only be taken to show that some people were living in the parish at that time, and not that there was still a nucleated settlement.

It is only by taking these many sources together and then applying the information given to the geography of the area, and our known social and archaeological history, that we can come to any conclusion as to the location and development of any village that we now consider 'lost'.

Gazetteer of Lost Villages

ALCISTON

NGR TQ505056

The street layout in this pretty village, which is first recorded in the Domesday Survey as 'Alsistone', is very much as it must have been in the medieval period, although the number of houses it contains has been considerably reduced. Like many place-names in this part of the county it relates to an enclosed settlement, or 'tun', belonging to an individual – in this case Aelfsige, a Saxon chieftain. Because the manor was owned for most of its recorded history by Battle Abbey it is better documented than many of its neighbours, and changes in the size of its population can be studied in conjunction with alterations in medieval agricultural practice.

At the time of the Domesday Survey there were 70 villagers, 8 smallholders and 12 slaves spread over a fairly large area. Two hundred years later, during the reign of Edward I, a total of 34 separate households are recorded – the majority of which would have been along the main street that survives today.

The Black Death of 1349 hit the village badly. The surviving Court Rolls for April that year record the deaths of 24 tenants – and as these would have been the heads of households, the actual death toll must have been considerably higher. By June sixteen plots of land that had previously been tenanted were in the hands of the Lord of the Manor, and a further 39 deaths were recorded. Although the majority of these people would have lived in the main settlement, we know that the manor also supported several outlying communities, whose figures are included in the total number of plague deaths, so it is possible that some of the more isolated hamlets were completely wiped out at this time.

This substantial depopulation was a blow for the monks of Battle

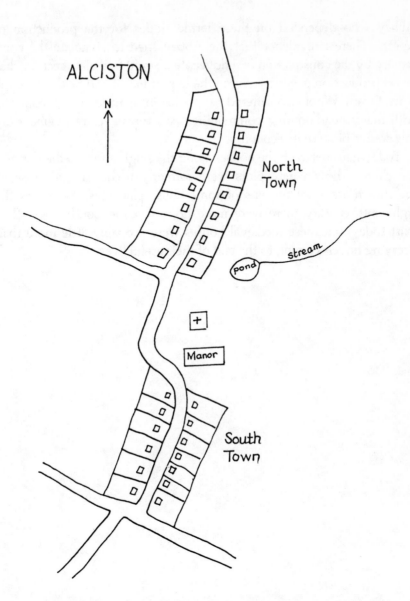

ALCISTON

N

North
Town

stream

pond

+

Manor

South
Town

A plan showing the extent of the village of Alciston in the medieval period. The
houses in the north town are now fewer in number, but the gaps can be clearly seen.
The south town has virtually disappeared.

Abbey who depended on these fertile slopes for the production of cereals. There is evidence that the Abbey tried to stimulate the community by the construction of a dovecote in 1368 (see plate section), but cereal production never recovered the importance it had held before the Black Death. Wool also suffered from a fall in demand, and in common with many neighbouring communities Alciston never recovered from this double blow to its economy.

Today gaps between the houses along the single street to the north of the church show where plots were formerly occupied, and close to the church are scant remains of some house platforms. As late as the eighteenth century there were more houses in the 'south town' than exist today, but these medieval houses were probably little more than decaying hovels coming to the end of their useful lives.

ALDRINGTON

NGR TQ266053

At the time of Domesday there were two main centres of population at Aldrington, with a total population of just over 60. These areas had at some stage belonged to a chieftain called Ealdhere, hence the name — Ealdhere's Tun, or enclosed farmstead. The nearby village of Aldringham also has the same derivation. The two centres each took account of the favourable geography of the area — one on the Adur estuary, the other on the wool-rich slopes of the lower Downs to the north. However, great coastal storms during the thirteenth and fourteenth centuries caused a loss of both agricultural land and houses. An inquisition of 1340 recorded the loss of 40 acres of coastal land, on which there had been an annual tithe charge of 20s. In addition to the erosion of their coastal lands the folk of Aldrington were suffering from the general depression caused by the drop in demand for wool, and both settlements went into rapid decline.

The church (see plate section), which had been situated in the northernmost settlement was already ruinous by the mid sixteenth century, when the then vicar took away the bell and font to save them from desecration.

An article in *The British Magazine* described what remained of the village in the early nineteenth century: 'In the neighbourhood of the bright sunshine and garish gaiety of a fashionable watering place, stand the unobserved ruins of Aldrington church, unapproached by any direct road; they are surrounded by green meadows, the sight of whose low and green surfaces brings an instant tranquillity and rest to the feelings, in which they are assisted by the soothing and monotonous sound of the sea, which is heard about half a mile distant. The leading character of this ruin (which is much strengthened by the surrounding champaign country) is that of unpretending simplicity. It is the remains of a village church, which in its completeness could offer nothing but its humility for our admiration; and the same simple character makes its impression in its decay. There is no slender pilaster, nor delicate mouldings, appealing to our love of grace and beauty – no lofty buttress to raise up feelings of grandeur and power; nor any gothic window, overgrown with ivy, to feed our senses with picturesque delight. Aldrington does not affect the imagination so much as the heart.'

Horsfield's *History of Sussex* (1835) records that priests were still appointed, although 'the only approach to religious worship (there) takes place at the induction of the rector'. At that time the rector was living at Penshurst in Kent!

The present church was built from the few surviving ruins of the old in 1878 as the western suburbs of Hove encroached on the area.

By the mid 17th century there were still two distinct parts to Aldrington – West Aldrington being near the sea with a few cottages, and East Aldrington near the church with just two houses recorded in the Hearth Tax Returns of the 1680s. In 1801, after the coastal cottages had been lost to the sea, the population of the entire parish was just two – the tollgate keeper and his wife – but following the rapid expansion of Hove the area became densely populated, and now forms an almost continuous community with two other settlements that had suffered complete depopulation, Hangleton and West Blatchington.

APULDRAM

NGR SU840033

To what extent Apuldram was ever a village is a little unclear. It does not appear in the Domesday Survey, but stands on what must have always been an important position on the eastern arm of the Chichester Channel – that busy waterway that had been in use from the time of the Roman occupation. During the reign of Henry I the manor was granted to the monks of Battle Abbey, so there must have been a useful income for them to have accepted it. The manor is first mentioned in a charter of the early twelfth century as 'Apeldreham', or 'homestead with apple trees'. This tends to imply that it was a single house rather than a nucleated settlement that was distinguished by apple trees. However, if there were no other houses in the locality it would not have been necessary to note the trees as a distinguishing feature, so it may be that Apuldram had some other houses.

In 1410 William Ryman built the house in Apuldram that now bears his name and today this and the Manor House more or less form the entire village, although there is a small early thirteenth century church nearby. For most of its history this formed a chapel of ease to nearby Bosham, serving the small community on the eastern side of the Chichester Channel, who would otherwise have had a difficult journey to their parish church. That it remained a chapel of ease, rather than a parish church in its own right, until the nineteenth century testifies to the small population here. Indeed for most of the medieval period the dead still had to be carried to Bosham for burial. If we assume a small population this would have been possible – but a large population would have had proportionally more deaths and after a while the sheer effort involved would have necessitated a change in the system to make Apuldram a parochial church.

In 1433 the monks of Battle Abbey surveyed Apuldram and found that it consisted of three streets – only one of which survives as a through road today. The main medieval road that served the small harbour for which this village was originally founded still runs towards

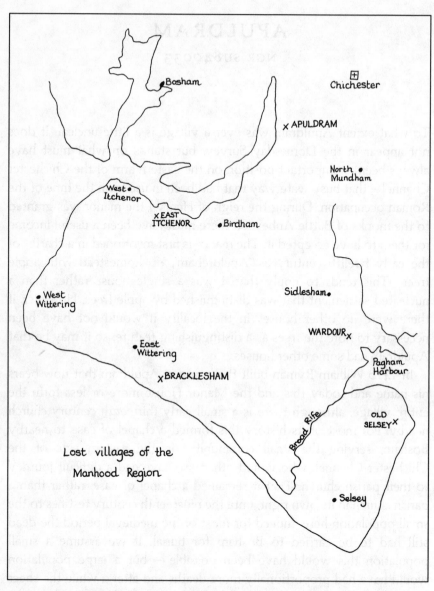

MAP OF THE MANHOOD REGION. Five deserted villages are to be found in this backwater in the south-western corner of the county.

the Manor House where it veers to the north, but it now becomes a footpath long before it reaches the water's edge, and the medieval harbour has been replaced by Dell Quay further to the south. This too, has declined since its late eighteenth century peak as a result of the construction of the Arundel and Portsmouth Canal a hundred and fifty years ago, although 18th and 19th century salt-panning filled a gap in the economy of the region.

The Black Death of 1349 hit villages that had a great deal of contact with other communities very badly, and the number of free agricultural workers in Apuldram was reduced from 234 to 168, and may have started the decline in population here that has continued until the present day.

ARLINGTON

NGR TQ542075

The Saxon church of St Pancras stands to the west of the present village. That the latter is a fairly recent settlement can be detected from the fact that most of the older houses in the parish are scattered across the surrounding farmland, and it seems likely that Arlington is an example of the type of settlement that was originally nucleated, gradually dispersed to service smallholdings, and which then came together again as a fairly compact village as the smallholdings were combined. At the time of Domesday the village was called 'Erlington', or the 'tun' (enclosed homestead) of an earl and his people. This does not mean that the unnamed earl lived here, but the fact that an enclosure is identified suggests that it was at that time a settled community within his estate.

The original village was situated to the south-west of the church (see plate section), where some extremely clear mounds and ditches – locally known as 'the sluices', indicate the plots formerly occupied by houses. Three buildings were still surviving in 1629 and are clearly marked on a map of 1629 in the County Record Office. In the mid seventeenth century the Religious Survey noted a total parish population of 211.

That the Black Death was not the reason for depopulation here is evidenced by the fact that Domesday records 5 villagers farming about 40 acres. In 1327 there were just 7 taxpayers, and it isn't until the seventeenth century that the population rises well into double figures. The foundation of Mickleham Priory a short distance to the north in 1229, and the grant of some woodland in the parish – still known as Abbot's Wood – to Battle Abbey during the reign of Henry I may have contributed to the movement of population away from a fixed settlement to a more scattered agricultural community.

BALMER

NGR TQ359100

There were several small farming communities on the wide open slopes of the Downs to the north of present day Brighton. The hamlet of Balmer, or Boromor, was one of them, situated within the ecclesiastical parish and manor of Falmer (see plate section). At the time of Domesday it comprised 4 hides – over 400 acres – and supported one villager, 2 smallholders and 2 slaves (tied tenants). Its name derives from the 'stronghold near the pool'. The latter may still be detected, and not far away can be seen the remains of early bank and ditch fortifications that would have pre-dated the more domestic settlements of this region.

This small hamlet had its own chapel, which was held by Lewes Priory until 1537. In that year it was handed to Cromwell's commissioners and probably demolished immediately. The 1563 Diocese of Chichester Survey makes no mention of a chapel here which suggests that it was no longer in existence. There is a field at Balmer called 'church laine', which may recall its former site.

The houses may have been built – as was common in the locality – around a pond, but only a few bumps in the ground have survived modern agricultural practice. Only one piece of old walling still stands, incorporated into a later house, although about a mile to the north the remains of an early field system may still be detected.

BALSDEAN

NGR TQ378059

The village of Balsdean was not recorded in the Domesday Survey, although excavations in 1953 proved that a settlement probably existed here at that time. The name derives from that of an early lord of the manor, Beald, plus a geographical position, valley, showing how important the sheltered location was to the early history of the site (see plate section).

Until the last war, when the area was occupied by the army, the remains of a small Norman church were still to be seen. From documentary sources it seems that this church was founded between 1121 and 1147, possibly by a member of the de Warenne family who held the manor. In about 1175 Hamelin de Warenne granted the manor, which comprised at that time of over 300 acres, to Lewes Priory, which had been founded a hundred years earlier by William de Warenne, one of William the Conqueror's most trusted commanders. Part of the grant probably provided the income for the precentor of the college at South Malling, who traditionally used Balsdean as a hunting estate.

As late as 1579 the vicar of Rottingdean was still charged to say service 4 times a year in the 'village of Balsdean' — a long climb over High Hill to this remote spot. The chapel was mentioned in a document of 1699, but by the eighteenth century had been abandoned. A watercolour in the Burrell Collection of the British Museum shows it in use as a farm building, with thatched roof and herringbone masonry (see plate section). The excavations proved the church to have been a small two cell building with an apsidal east end. Interestingly it appeared to have been built on a site that had previously been occupied, and a small twelfth century book clasp was among the items to be discovered.

Today nothing of any antiquity survives at Balsdean.

BARCOMBE

NGR TQ418143

That this place was named after the popular medieval cereal crop growing here – barley – shows us that this part of the Ouse valley has long
been used for arable farming. The combe in the name does not, ap-
parently, derive from the word for valley, but from the Old English
word 'camp', meaning 'field'. There is little evidence to show what hap-
pened to the original village – or when – although at the time of
Domesday it seems that there were over 1000 acres supporting 24
villagers and 2 smallholders.

During the late thirteenth and early fourteenth centuries the village
must have been fairly prosperous as the church was substantially rebuilt
at that time, although subsequent restoration in the nineteenth century
has robbed it of the patina of years. Both the main and west doors, and
the aisle arcades are of this date, as is the font. To have undertaken this
large scale rebuilding at more or less the same time would have required
a considerable amount of income.

In front of the church is the Penance Pond – which it has been
suggested was so named after witches were dunked in it. Yet is it not
feasible that the penance refers to the locals' horror at the Black Death of
1349 which they saw as a warning from God? It seems likely that the
subsequent reduction in population led to much land going to waste and
the virtual abandonment of a proper settlement. The field where the
houses would have stood – between the church and river – would not
have been an ideal site and, like nearby Hamsey, would probably have
been abandoned at a later date in any case.

The river was navigable up to Barcombe, but the lack of suitable land
for building adjacent to the river meant that it was never developed to
its full potential, and today the main settlement is to be found at Barcombe Cross, some distance to the north.

BARNHORNE

NGR TQ705076

The manor of Barnhorne from which this medieval settlement took its name stood on a hook of land which jutted into Pevensey Bay to the south of Hooe. The 'horne' in the name refers directly to the shape of the piece of land, whilst the barn participle derives straight from 'barley', the primary crop in these parts.

It was owned, like many other local manors, for much of its history by the monks of Battle Abbey, and their regular surveys and assessments tell us much about the development of this predominantly arable settlement.

The original manor was situated just to the north of Rokes Wood which survives today next to the A259 coastal road. It must have been replaced by 1305 as in that year the former site is referred to as the 'old town'. This date coincides nicely with the reclamation work undertaken by the Abbey amidst the tidal marshes of Pevensey Bay. Drainage channels were constructed and sea walls erected to create further land for cereal crops. Large numbers of people were required – not just to reclaim and farm the area, but also to keep it free from flooding during the severe winter storms that destroyed so many settlements along the south coast.

The new Barnhorne was situated further to the south and west of the former settlement, at a point in the fields now marked by the junction of three footpaths. Ploughing has now destroyed any remains of house platforms, although rights of way clearly indicate the former layout of the road system here.

The exact reason for depopulation at a fairly early stage is not known, although it was probably a combination of the Black Death, coastal storms and a change away from cereal production to less labour-intensive livestock farming, all of which had a major impact in Sussex during the fourteenth century.

BEDDINGHAM

NGR TQ445078

Beddingham is a very early settlement, first mentioned at the start of the ninth century, when it was spelt Beadyngham. This is the farming settlement of Beald, who is probably the same person who gave his name to the other deserted village of Balsdean not so far away. It stands close to the famous Iron Age hill-fort of Mount Caburn and not far from the Bronze Age village at Itford Hill. In these geographical locations early valley settlements often developed in the lee of the hill-forts, close to rivers and their strategic crossings. Domesday Book records the existence of four salt pans in the eleventh century, indicating a community based not solely on agriculture.

Here in the valley of the Ouse the fertile soil lent itself to arable farming, and several settlements grew up along the edge of the flood plain. Beddingham seems to have been at a slight advantage in that it stood at the junction of the main valley and a cross valley that now carries the A27, and was able to benefit from a certain amount of communication denied the more remote settlements on the steep slope of the downs to the south.

A track to the south and west of the church, which is Norman in origin, seems to indicate the position of lost houses, although it is not clear how long ago they vanished. That the present church was still under construction in the sixteenth century indicates either a long slow period of construction, or a sudden burst of activity occasioned by new-found wealth. The latter is probably more accurate as it ties in with the date of Cobbe Place, a late sixteenth century house some distance to the south of the vanished village.

BINDERTON
NGR SU851108

Binderton House, which lies to the south of West Dean, stands on the site of the medieval village of Binderton which at the time of Domesday Book was assessed at 3 hides – about 300 acres. At that time it supported 8 villagers and 9 smallholders and there was a church. The name contains a female personal name – Beornpryp – plus the familiar 'tun', or enclosure round a homestead. For much of its history the Manor was owned by Tarrant Abbey in Dorset, to whom it had been granted on behalf of Queen Eleanor who had acquired the property in the late thirteenth century. Following the Reformation the manor was granted to its long-standing tenants, the Smith family, and it was they who built the present house in 1677.

By this time the church, which consisted of nave and chancel only, was proving difficult to maintain and Thomas Smith, finding that it would interfere with the view from his new house, pulled it down in about 1671 and built a replacement on the other side of the road.

In 1611 it had been reported that the chancel roof had collapsed. That it was repaired shortly afterwards is evident from the churchwarden's report of 1640 in which they stated that 'noe part of our church is demolished, nor put to any profane use'. However, once Mr Smith had decided that the old church was in his way it didn't take long for him to convince the churchwardens that a new church would be easier to maintain.

As it happens, this new church – a simple rectangle built of flint and brick – was never completed and soon fell into decay. The population of Binderton in the seventeenth century (19 adults in 1641) was barely more than the occupants of Binderton House, and the needs of the parishioners could easily be served by the priest from nearby West Dean. An interesting letter of 1687 survives in the Bodleian Library from the then Bishop of Chichester to the Archbishop of Canterbury asking what the official line on the unfinished church was. Before matters were resolved Thomas Smith died and had to be buried in the family vault of the incomplete church.

The presence of hill-forts and earthworks in the area are indicative of a moving population over at least two thousand years — a small population always able to adapt to changes in social and economic fortune by moving within the manorial boundaries much easier than a large one.

BINSTED
NGR TQ982061

At the time of Domesday there were 4 hides of land here (over 400 acres) supporting at least eight households. That the population never grew to the extent of being wealthy is shown by the small two-cell Norman church which stands on the lane that leads from the north. The church contains much of interest including a twelfth century font.

Records are extremely slight, other than the fact that Tortington Priory near Arundel held the manor, but the location of Binsted, near to other known depopulated sites suggests that the particular geographical and climatic conditions of the region were primarily to blame for the abandonment of traditional sites during the first five hundred years of their existence. The area was 'out on a limb' and had heavy soil unsuitable for cereal production. Later on this was turned to some benefit as medieval tile and pottery kilns have been discovered – yet these were not profitable enough to sustain a complete village.

We have very little other evidence on which to work – including the problematic place name – which simply means the 'place where beans grow'. There must have been many places in this part of Sussex where such a crop was cultivated, so why this one was singled out to identify it from the others is not certain. To the north of the church is a flat meadow that is certainly large enough to have supported permanent or semi-permanent buildings that would have housed the Domesday population and room for limited arable farming.

BODIAM

NGR TQ785259

Bodiam presents a few problems for the historian. The famous Castle, founded by Sir Edward Dalyngrydge, Keeper of the Tower of London, in 1385, stands at the opposite end of the present village to the parish church. Sir Edward sought permission of the Crown to embattle his 'manor by the sea', for the Rother was navigable this far north. That he was fond of this area and saw both financial and military benefits by the development of the site is clear from the fact that he also obtained a charter for a weekly Saturday market. The French had already made incursions into the county and Dalyngrydge's castle would have been in a strategically sensitive location. It would have required a large population to service it, and it seems there were once houses close to the Castle moat, of which some field marks may still be detected. Horsfield's *History of Sussex* suggests that the manorial lands were formerly more extensive than the present parochial boundary.

Before the construction of the Castle the original Manor House stood to the north-east of the church – its moat may still be seen, and it is probable that the area between this and the church was the site of the first settlement. As the place name suggests it was a homestead – or ham – of Boda a Norman moneyer. After the grant of the charter for both a market and fair in the early 14th century it is likely that the village expanded to the south of the church – an expansion that was physically limited by the construction of the Castle.

The Castle saw no action against the French, and was little more than a farmhouse by the 17th century when it was abandoned.

BOTOLPHS

NGR TQ194092

The village of Botolphs does not appear under this name in the Domesday Survey. It has taken the name of its church following the loss of the original village after the Black Death.

The original name of this community was Annington, which at the time of Domesday had 15 villagers, 34 smallholders and a church (see plate section). Over 600 acres of fertile river valley were under cultivation, and the church stood at the end of a short village street that then descended to the River Adur, where there was a small wharf, which may still be identified from Ordnance Survey maps today.

It seems more than likely that the depopulation occurred soon after the Black Death. The major evidence to support this is the fabric of the parish church itself. Botolphs is a medium sized church of early eleventh century origin, which was much enlarged by the addition of a north aisle in the late thirteenth century. Soon afterwards this was removed and the arcade which separated it from the nave was blocked in – leaving the row of arches we clearly see today. These structural alterations are often our only tangible evidence of changes in medieval prosperity – from a large population to a much smaller one that had to make allowances for its diminished circumstances.

Apart from the church, the only evidence of the former settlement is the former manor house to the west, and some lumps and bumps in the fields between the two.

BRACKLESHAM

NGR SZ805964

Because Bracklesham was a sub-manor of other settlements in the Manhood region few records survive of the medieval village, which now lies
under the sea (see map on page 20). However we are able to judge
something from the place-name which incorporates the familiar 'ham' or
unenclosed homestead. This is usually preceded by a personal name,
either that of the chieftain or an early individual settler. In this case,
because of its proximity to the sea, it has been suggested that it is
derived from the popular Scandinavian name Breaha.   Its two neighbours, East Wittering and Earnley have kept their old churches as they
were built some way inland, but all traces of medieval Bracklesham have
disappeared completely. The present settlement of the same name is
primarily of mid twentieth century origins, associated with the development of the area as a holiday and retirement resort.

BROOMHILL

NGR TQ988183

The village of Broomhill stood to the east of the Rother Estuary and its site is marked on Stonham's map of 1599 as 'Promehill'. That map showed several embankments which W. MacLean, writing in 1938, could still identify, although there is little evidence of the existence of a hill of any sort here, and even less of the broom that must have grown on it at some time. The highest land in the former parish is sixteen feet about sea level. Of all the deserted villages in this book, Broomhill strikes one as being in the most inhospitable area possible.

The small town was lost during the same storm that swept away neighbouring Winchelsea in 1287. The church, which was probably the only permanent stone building to survive the storm, was a ruin by 1637, and its site has recently been excavated, although detailed results have yet to be published. The landscape here is one of the most exposed in the county – acres of low flat land with little protection from the elements other than the sea wall to the south. The area is probably even less densely populated now – even taking into account the twentieth century housing – than it was in the Middle Ages, when more people were required to service the land.

A commission of 1377 was formed to inspect the marshland embankment 'from the town of Romney to Promhill church'. To the south of Broomhill on the coast stood a small religious house or independent hermitage which maintained a beacon to direct shipping into the Harbour that served the town of Rye.

Most of the marshland hereabouts was owned in the Middle Ages by the Abbeys of Battle and Robertsbridge, and it was recorded in 1333 that the latter had lost several hundred pounds of annual income as a result of the sea taking their land. It is possible that these inundations resulted in the settlement of Broomhill regularly moving around within its manorial boundaries, as a charter of 1309 records 'Eadle Promhelle' as a boundary mark.

BULVERHYTHE

NGR TQ768082

Bulverhythe seems not to have been mentioned in Domesday, but is found in the records of the Cinque Ports from the thirteenth century onwards, when it was a non-Corporate member of the Confederation, attached to Hastings. Hythe is a common name in England which always relates to a landing place. Here it is partnered with Bulver which had its origins in the Old English word 'burg' which denotes a fortification. This suggests that although the settlement was established to provide a safe harbour and port for Hastings – which did not enjoy a particularly sheltered position, it was constructed near an existing fortification. As a result of its links with Hastings Bulverhythe shared that town's rights and privileges, as a member of the Cinque Ports Confederation, in return for secure mooring rights.

No doubt its early life was that of a plain landing stage and quay, but as a resident population developed so other requirements became apparent, in particular a parish church. This was established by 1372, and stood some way inland from the harbour, and consisted of a two cell church with a short west tower that may have been used for navigational purposes. A market was also established, together with a ferry service across the harbour mouth, both of which indicate a not insubstantial population.

The records of the port are rather scanty, but they do show that it was still busy in 1500, and just working in the 17th century when the coastline started to change rapidly, at first silting up the entrance channel, and finally eroding the harbour away altogether. In 1831 the population of Bulverhythe was just 51 – the three principal buildings in the parish being the Bull Inn and two Martello Towers!

What few medieval houses survived the storms have disappeared, and today the only surviving evidence of early Bulverhythe are two small pieces of flint wall that formed part of the parish church standing in Hythe Avenue, surrounded by twentieth century housing (see plate section).

BURPHAM

NGR 040088

The village of Burpham is a good example of a settlement that has shifted from its original location – albeit by just a few hundred yards, and its place name – the 'ham' by the 'burg' – indicates the direction of the move from a fortified site to an unenclosed homestead. There may have been an Iron Age fort here, on a small promontory overlooking the River Arun, but the promontory reached its greatest period under King Alfred who established a burg, or fortified site here in about 720. This was to protect the coastal plains from the threat of a Danish invasion, and was one of several similar structures constructed along the south coast.

The area inside the enclosure was reported to have been large enough to support over 700 households, although that was probably an over-statement. The outer earthen banks may be seen very clearly today (see plate section), and it is difficult to believe that there were originally houses inside the fortifications. Excavations have proved the existence of foundations of Saxon timber-framed houses, at least just inside the main eastern entrance into the fort.

When the Normans came to settle here they took advantage of a slightly sheltered hill to the east of the entrance on which to build their church. This is an excellent survivor of about 1150, and around this the new village grew. Probably by this time the Saxon fort had been entirely depopulated in favour of a site that was not quite as isolated and difficult of access.

BURPHAM

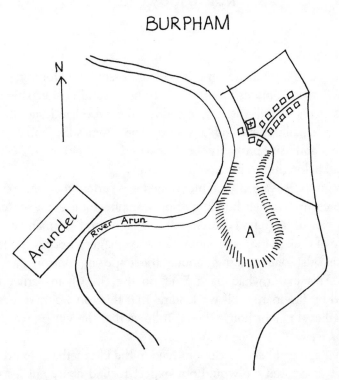

Plan showing how the early Saxon settlement at Burpham moved from the Burgh 'A' to the unprotected site to the north.

BURTON

NGR TQ967176

In contrast to many villages in this part of Sussex, the Domesday Book entry for Burton conjures up a picture of hustle and bustle. There were over 500 acres, a mill, fishery, meadow and woodland supporting 8 villagers, 3 smallholders and 2 slaves. The Domesday entry is spelt Bongetune and can probably be translated as the tun, or enclosed homestead belonging to Buna.

Although there is no church mentioned it is certain that one existed – for the present two-cell building shows architectural evidence of that period. It was usual to find churches of the Saxon and Norman periods at the centre of their manor, surrounded by the villagers' houses. Today the church has just one near neighbour, the imposing Burton Park built in 1831. This in turn had been built on the site of an earlier house destroyed by fire in 1826. If we assume that this too was the successor of the medieval manor house then it follows that the village was in this vicinity as well.

If the village had been forcibly moved in the Elizabethan period when the park was created we would not expect to find many entries in the Hearth Tax returns of the 17th century. Indeed this is the case. Furthermore, lack of alterations in the architecture of the church also suggest that the movement, or in any case the depopulation, of Burton had taken place much earlier that the Elizabethan period, and had little to do with the creation of the park.

BUXTED

NGR TQ486231

In a county where the majority of lost villages disappeared as a result of changes in agricultural practice at about the time of the Black Death, it is rare to find other factors coming into play.

The medieval village of Buxted – which does not appear in the Domesday Survey – and which takes it name from 'the place where box trees grow' – stood to either end of the thirteenth century church, as a linear development. It seems to have been abandoned in the eighteenth century when Thomas Medley pulled down the old manor house and built the present mansion on a site close to the south side of the church. To provide a parkland setting the village was moved further to the north east. The move was made 'official' in the nineteenth century when the

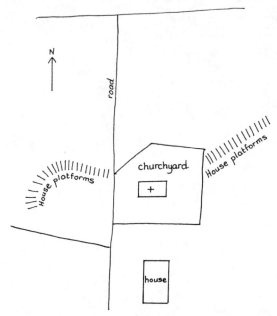

Plan to show the position of the medieval house platforms at Buxted in relation to the medieval church and later mansion house. When the churchyard was extended further remains were destroyed.

railway passed through the area and encouraged even more development.

Some eighteenth century prints show a few houses standing near the church, but today the only signs of former habitation are some noticeable house platforms due west and north east of the church (see plate section). When pipes were being laid in 1968 the village well was discovered to the west of the church tower. It is probable that the two visible sections of street continued over the line of the present north churchyard wall. Fieldwalking in 1978 produced a large amount of pottery and other artefacts from the medieval period onwards.

The setting of the surviving house platforms is one of great beauty. The parkland setting is wonderfully maintained, and helps to show off the surviving fieldmarks to the greatest advantage, making Buxted one of the best places in the county to start a study of lost medieval villages.

CHILGROVE

NGR SU834158

Partial excavation in 1977 identified the remains of the chapel of Chilgrove, some miles to the north of the present village of that name. Chil is derived from the Old English for 'throat', or 'neck', which in this case must relate to the narrow valley that provided the location for the original settlement, and which at the time the village needed to be identified was filled with a grove of trees.

The chapel had first been mentioned in 1210, and existed in use until the sixteenth century when it fell into disrepair. Certainly from 1602 onwards the parishioners worshipped at West Dean church.

The remains of the chapel were found to be of a two-cell church with eastern apse, similar in style to other known 11th and 12th century buildings in the county.

The loss of the chapel has been linked to the disappearance of the hamlet of Chilgrove, a short distance to the north-west. This was probably a linear development of about a dozen houses built on artificial platforms up the side of this very narrow sheltered valley. It is just possible that the construction of nearby Monkton Farm and subsequent changes in agricultural practice led to the abandonment of this settlement in the late 16th or early 17th centuries. The very name – Monkton – survives from the early history of the hamlet, which belonged to the monks of Waverley Abbey in Surrey for much of its recorded history.

CHINGTON
NGR TQ508985

Substantial remains discovered at Chington Farm were thought to be part of a failed new town, built to replace the decaying Seaford shortly after 1347 when the Manor passed from the de Warenne family to the Poynings. The 'tun', or enclosed homestead, of the Cintingas tribe, formerly stood here and was seen as the ideal location for the new town. After all it had supported habitation for at least three hundred years, and it was far better to establish a new town on a proven site rather than risk a green field location.

No documentary evidence shows why this new town was unsuccessful, but in 1854 M.A. Lower claimed that remains discovered on site showed signs of burning – so it is possible that French raids in the latter part of the fourteenth century put paid to the settlement.

As a medieval chapel is recorded here, and mention is made of Chington in a document of 1321, the choice of an established community – albeit a small one – for the new town was obviously an attempt to ensure rapid success. The site is open and fairly flat, and may have meant to make use of the estuary of the River Cuckmere as a natural harbour in place of the Ouse at Seaford, which was rapidly moving to the west.

In the archives of Althorp a deed survives recording the sale of the Lordship of the Manor, in 1445, from Henry Earl of Northumberland to Sir Edward Seymour.

COOMBES

NGR TQ191082

The valley from which this picturesque settlement takes its name is a steep and narrow dell to the west of the valley of the River Adur (see plate section). At the time of Domesday the Manor had over 500 acres of land supporting 27 villagers, 4 smallholders and 2 slaves. In addition to a church there was also a salthouse.

There is no doubt that the location for the village was ideal. The hills to the south and west formed a natural shelter and were eminently suitable for grazing sheep. The river offered easy communication, fishing, and perhaps even scope for small local industries such as boat-building.

Today the church is the earliest survival – a two cell building of late eleventh century date displaying some exceptional wall paintings and contemporary stone carvings. The building itself is constructed into the hillside, its east end possibly standing on an artificial platform.

Little remains of the village – although an early estate map shows more houses to the east of the church than exist today. We can only guess that agricultural changes, together with the effects of the Black Death and the isolated position of the village all led to a gradual decline, very similar to that of the nearby manor of Annington (see Botolphs).

DUNCTON

NGR TQ960170

The village of Duncton has moved slightly from its medieval position, which seems to have been a little to the south of the present settlement. The main road between Petworth and Chichester is a fairly recent addition to the landscape – the downland in this locality offering very steep and difficult terrain. The Turnpike Acts for its establishment at this point date from 1757. A few miles to the south the Roman Stane Street crosses the county on a much easier alignment. Roman remains have been discovered in Duncton, showing a continuity of settlement not often found in this part of Sussex.

The medieval manor of Duncton, or 'Dunnucca's tun', as recorded in the Domesday Book, comprised 15 villagers, 8 smallholders, a church, 4 mills and 2 fisheries. The latter were probably situated near the centre of population at a point where the stream running through the valley could be dammed. The lines of communication which formerly ran east/west linking Burton and East Lavington, and which is still preserved in part as the drive of Seaford College, would have taken in the village of Duncton.

For much of its medieval history Duncton church formed a chapel of ease to Petworth, and does not have as many surviving records as other neighbouring parishes.

EAST ITCHENOR

NGR SU801005

For there to be a West Itchenor one would expect there to be an East Itchenor — but none exists on a modern map. Today the village of Birdham is the nearest medieval survivor to the east of West Itchenor, but formerly the gap between them was occupied by East Itchenor, recorded in the Domesday Survey (see map on page 20). The name Itchenor derives from the Old English for 'river bank', *ora*, prefixed by the personal name of the settler, who in this case was Ycca. As the first documentary evidence of these places is in a charter of AD683 we can be sure that this southern bank of the Chichester Channel has been in use as a landing place for at least 1500 years.

In a 1291 survey East Itchenor rectory was valued at £8.00 a year, as opposed to Birdham's £5.6s.8d. Its income probably derived from both trading and agriculture.

If one assumes that both the Itchenor's were used as landing places on the southern side of the Chichester Channel, then it seems obvious that they were too close together to be commercially viable. There were two geographic advantages to being situated on the western side — a crossing place to Bosham, in a position less affected by silting on a bend. One had to lose out in time.

Early in the thirteenth century there was a dispute between the rector of East Itchenor and his parishioners in which a chapel at Cowdray was mentioned. Today there is a Cowdray Farm to the north-east of Birdham — indicating that this may have been in, or near, the parish. There is also a very strange footpath layout between West Itchenor and Birdham which may indicate early rights of way.

By 1441 the population of East Itchenor had declined to such an extent that the parish was united with that of Birdham, and East Itchenor church was allowed to become ruinous. It was finally demolished in the eighteenth century, and there do not seem to be any other surviving features of this once lively settlement.

EXCEAT

NGR TQ522992

The disappearance of Exceat seems to have taken place slightly later than other settlements in this part of the county, and may not have been affected by the Black Death to the same extent.

At the time of Domesday the manor was divided into two sections – one of two-and-a-half hides supporting 7 smallholders, the other of four-and-a-half hides supporting three villagers, 6 smallholders and a slave. Although no church is mentioned in the Survey it seems likely that one existed – as excavations in 1916 indicated that the surviving foundations were probably of early Norman date. It stood in the part of the parish that gave the place its name – the Oak Grove – on the sheltered bank away from the exposed valley of the Cuckmere (see plate section).

Documentary sources are scarce, but in 1460 we learn that only two houses existed, and that the church was in ruins. This late date suggests that other houses had disappeared in living memory, and points to the frequent French raids of the late fourteenth century as being the most likely cause for depopulation. We know from other sources that these severely affected other nearby places, and it would be hard to imagine that the village of Exceat, only a little way up the hillside from the wide valley of the River Cuckmere, could have escaped. Many villagers would probably have moved to safer locations, leaving those who had decided to stay to take over their plots of land. A record of 1404 records the acquisition of five tenements by John Wolf. It would only take a couple of these takeovers to ensure that the village could never be repopulated.

In 1528 the parish of Exceat was united to that of West Dean, a short distance to the east, and today this part of the valley is well-known, having been turned into a Country Park with excellent visitor facilities.

FORD

NGR TQOO2037

Ford marked one of the lowest crossing places of the River Arun, although it was never as well-used as the defended crossing point at Arundel. The settlement was not recorded in the Domesday Book, although it must have been in existence, as the present isolated church shows evidence of Norman work (see plate section).

Until the construction of the Portsmouth and Arundel Canal in 1818 there were many humps and bumps adjacent to the church which were said to be the remains of a medieval settlement. Those that survived the building work – and its subsequent closure and infilling- have been partially excavated, and have been shown to be the foundations of medieval buildings and their associated boundaries. One of the foundations was undoubtedly that of the manor house – suggesting the typical Sussex plan of a nucleated settlement of church, manor and cottages.

The 1525 Lay Subsidy Rolls suggest a lively population – but by the 17th century Hearth Tax returns the village seems to have been deserted. This may have been the result of the enclosure of grazing lands and a slow move from a nucleated settlement under common occupation to that of isolated smallholdings of the yeoman farmers in the area.

GLATTING

NGR TQ972142

Glatting is yet another example of depopulation in the slopes to the north of the South Downs. A little further away are the deserted villages of Duncton and Burton. Whenever we find '-ing' as part of a place name we can be sure that this was a settlement of Scandinavian origin, often prefixed by a personal name, in this case a man called Glott.

Life must always have been difficult here. Domesday records 400 acres of land supporting just 3 villagers and 2 smallholders. The land here is not of the best quality, and varies from light downland with little soil cover to the heavy valley clays. The lack of early through roads at this point would have made it difficult to encourage a viable market, and other well-established settlements on better trade routes would have been an irresistible draw to those in the area.

HAMSEY

NGR TQ414122

This village stood on a hill in a bend of the Ouse. As a particularly fertile plain it supported 13 hides of land in the Domesday Survey, in which the village is recorded as plain Hamm – the Say family, later lords of the manor, didn't take up residence until the thirteenth century, when the present place-name was adopted.

The population now lives primarily to the west and north – on the valley slopes. The move was probably occasioned by the fact that as the village expanded it outgrew the narrow hill on which it had been established (see plate section). Whilst it would have been possible to build on the flat plain of the valley floor, this was extremely low lying land and subject to almost annual flooding.

It seems that the manor house stood on the small piece of slightly higher land to the east of the church, and that the foundations were still visible in the eighteenth century. The contract for its erection, in 1321, is still in existence in Westminster Abbey's archives and gives much detail about its size – 30 feet by 90 feet – and the surprising fact that it had two fireplaces in the great hall – almost unheard of at this early date. Whilst the site of the former village has never been fully excavated pieces of slate found on the surface have been identified as coming from South Devon – a sure indicator that the Ouse was an important channel for communication, and must have been a contributory factor to the village being established here in the first instance. It was also important as a fishery – in 1237 William de Say granted fishing rights in the manor to Earl Warenne.

The abandonment of Hamsey is probably contemporary with that of Barcombe, some distance to the north.

HANGLETON

NGR TQ268074

Today this is a densely populated area, but until 1952 only the church
and a few houses survived from the medieval settlement that was first
mentioned in Domesday. At that time there were 31 villagers and 13
smallholders with in excess of a thousand acres.

The medieval church of St Helen stands on what was once a main
road running along the escarpment in a westerly direction towards
Portslade, and would have stood at the centre of its village (see plate
section). The escarpment features prominently in the place-name 'hangle'
in Old English, meaning a 'slope'. With the 'tun', or enclosed settlement,
we can be fairly certain that the original settlement stood on the hillside.

Depopulation took place here prior to the Black Death. In 1339 an
Inquisition at Poynings recorded that a dovecote had become ruinous,
and the following year it was recorded that 'several lands were barren
and uncultivated'. Yet a hundred years earlier the population had been
wealthy enough to add a tower to their church and to rebuild the
chancel.

It is obvious that the depopulation was brought about by changes in
agricultural practice in the early part of the fourteenth century, and
compounded by the Black Death, for in 1428 only two households are
recorded. Having changed from arable farming to sheep production the
surviving population was then knocked back when the price for fleeces
dropped.

In the early sixteenth century Richard Scrase, 'Gentleman', of
Hangleton, left in his will the manors of Hangleton and Midtown to his
son James. Between them these manors then contained 1400 sheep, 100
oxen and 2 ploughs.

The Hearth Tax returns of mid seventeenth century date record five
houses − 2 large (Hangleton Place and Benfield Place) and 3 small.
Examination in the 1950s at Hangleton revealed the manor house to
have been of 15th century date, and the few village houses that were
excavated were shown to be single storey medieval dwellings in which

animals and humans coexisted. They were roofed using the same slates from South Devon that have been discovered in other deserted villages – such as Erringham and Hamsey.

HEENE

NGR TQ138027

Heene is mentioned in the Domesday Book and at that time contained 3 villagers and 2 smallholders. That it was then under arable cultivation is evidenced by the mention in the entry of a plough – and the place name itself (which is the subject of much speculation) possibly shows that hay or straw was produced here.

Heene marked the medieval western boundary of the harbour rights of the Port of Shoreham, so was often mentioned, but never described, in documentary sources. Its parish registers commence in 1594, but almost from the start were incorporated in those of West Tarring. G.D. Johnston, writing in *Sussex Notes and Queries* in 1950 suggested that the church must have become a ruin when the sea encroached in the early years of the sixteenth century.

Today the area is densely populated and all evidence of the fertile land on the slopes of the downs has disappeared. Further to the east the settlement of Hangleton (see separate entry) occupies an almost identical south-facing slope.

HEIGHTON ST CLERE

NGR TQ478075

A small village – not recorded in the Domesday Survey – stood in what is now the park of Firle Place. The main source for the size of the village is the series of subsidy returns of fourteenth to sixteenth century date. These show a taxable population of over two dozen people. Heighton derives its name from its topographical position – the 'tun by the height' – as it stands to the north of the South Downs escarpment.

In the late fifteenth century Eleanor St Clere married Sir John Gage who came from a West Country family. Their son William Gage married Agnes Bolney who owned the neighbouring manor of Firle. This marriage united the two manors and a large estate was thus created – which only required one manor house. During William's lifetime (he died in 1496) the manor of Heighton was abandoned in favour of that at Firle where a start was made on a new house. No doubt the houses that stood around the old Heighton Manor were gradually abandoned in favour of an enlarged community at Firle.

Today a few lumps and bumps survive in the park to the east of Firle Place together with what appears to be a silted pond, but no excavations have been undertaken. These are probably the remains of Heighton, although to confuse the historian there are mentions of a place called East Firle in the thirteenth century. Possibly they were one and the same.

HERSTMONCEUX

NGR TQ643103

The present village stands some distance to the north of the medieval church and castle. From the Domesday Survey and later tax returns we find a sizeable population, and it seems likely that this would have been a nucleated community situated near the church. In our early language a 'herst', variously spelled, was always a 'light wood on dry ground', and here it was owned during the twelfth and thirteenth centuries by the Monceux family, whose main seat was at Monceaux in Normandy. They had acquired the manor through marriage – and are best remembered for their support given to Simon de Montfort in the mid thirteenth century. By the early 14th century the male line had died out, and the Fiennes family came into possession.

Although there are no visible signs of a medieval community there now we know that the manor was emparked by Roger Fenys in 1441, and this emparkation may have taken in the site of the former settlement, forcing a move to the north. A survey undertaken in 1570 describes Herstmonceux as follows:

'The Park standeth on the east side of the church, being three miles about, the third part thereof lying in lawns, the residence well set with great timber trees, most of beech and partly oak, of fair timber. The game of fallow deer in the same park are by estimation two hundred. There are four fair ponds well replenished with carp, tenche etc., and four stewes besides the mote being dry. There is a hernery (heronry) in the same park called the Hern-Wood, the same hath yielded this year one hundred and fifty nests. There is a fair warren of conies . . . the same game being of late in the keeping of the keeper for the yearly rent of £6 13s 4d. There is a lodge covered in thack, and a stable very ruinous in timber and covering wherein the keeper now lyeth. There are two highways leading through the Park to the church market and townshipps adjacent'

HYDNEYE

NGR TQ609028

Hydneye was a non-corporate member of the Cinque Ports Confederation attached to the Port of Hastings. Several thirteenth and fourteenth century charters mention people from this village – who were able to enjoy the many benefits of Cinque Port membership- but no reliable population figures are available.

The settlement was situated in what is now the Hampden Park area of Eastbourne, where the small stream that enters the coast at The Crumbles formed a natural inlet. Its place name indicates that the settlement was situated on an island (the 'eye') that covered about a hide of land – 120 acres.

This inlet is now completely blocked by huge shingle banks and it was this natural blockage, helped along by severe coastal storms in the fourteenth century, that caused the abandonment of Hydneye. The first edition Ordnance Survey 6in. map shows the medieval road layout that survived until twentieth century development destroyed it, and the remains of its medieval church.

ISLESHAM

NGR TQ009001

Islesham stood approximately three miles west of Littlehampton and is one of several Sussex villages that have completely disappeared as a result of coastal erosion. Records are very scarce, but it seems that it in the Middle Ages it formed part of the lands belonging to Seez Abbey in France. That it was a farming settlement can be seen from the suffix '-ham', prefixed by the personal name Gisla. In Domesday Book it is shown as Gisleham.

Today, Bailiffscourt contains the sole surviving medieval building along this part of exposed coast. This was the house of the bailiff of the manor – whose job it was to oversee the management of these outlying lands. The chapel survives from the bailiff's house, but most of the present hotel dates from a scholarly building project of the 1930s to create a 'new' medieval house.

LINCH

NGR TQ849185

This rural village, now represented by Linch Farm to the west of Bepton, was mentioned in Domesday Book as having a church. This stood to the west of the present house — its location having been identified by the discovery of large numbers of human bones in the last century. Its rather strange place name comes directly from the Old English 'hlinc', meaning a hill.

From the value attached to the church we can see how dramatically the area declined in prosperity. In 1291 it was worth £5.6s.8d a year, a figure which fell to £4 a year over the next two centuries. In 1428 there were 6 householders and a rectory.

In the sixteenth century priests were still being appointed to Linch, although they no longer served the original church, for a chapel of ease had been built some miles to the north where an outlying portion of the parish at Woodsmangreen supported a larger population. This was a typical arrangement in Sussex which allowed for movement of cattle from the main settlements in the south to their grazing lands in the north.

These grazing lands were usually clearings in the Wealden forest that were linked to their base villages by drove-ways — wide, straight tracks that invariably run north-south. Many of these tracks are still in use today, several having been converted into main roads. In 1713 the rector, Henry Baker, had no parsonage and lived at Fernhurst. There were no tithes to support him, but Lord Montague, who at that time held the patronage, paid him £22.00 per year towards his expenses.

LORDINGTON

NGR TQ782098

Lordington stands in the parish of another deserted medieval village, Racton. Yet unlike Racton it has lost even its chapel, whose charge was united to that of Racton in 1445 when it became clear that the revenues necessary to sustain two centres of worship were no longer being raised. This is a sure sign that changes in agricultural practice, and the effects of the Black Death, had led to a sharp decline in population. There does not appear to be a connection between the village and any single Lord who could have given the 'enclosed homestead' its name, and the prefix 'Lord' probably comes from a personal name rather than a title.

In the thirteenth century there were several disputes between the Abbey at Lewes and the Beauchamp family as to who had the right of presentation to Lordington church. The more powerful Abbey won their case by stating that the church was a chapel of ease within their parish of Stoughton, and not an independent chapel to Racton!

At the time of Domesday there were over 500 acres of land at Lordington, with 8 villagers, 7 smallholders, 2 slaves and a mill. The houses probably stood on the site of the present Lordington Farm, on the east-facing slopes of a narrow valley, with the stream that would have powered the mill running nearby.

LULLINGTON

NGR TQ528031

Because of its tiny picturesque church in an isolated downland position, Lullington is one of the most famous deserted villages in Sussex (see plate section). Lullington receives no mention in the Domesday Survey, and derives its name from the 'enclosed settlement' of Lulla, probably a Saxon tenant. Its church is first recorded in 1249, although recent archaeological excavations have proved that the church must have been there at least a hundred years earlier. Contrary to popular opinion this is not the smallest church in England, as it is only a fragment of a much larger structure. This in itself is first rate evidence that the prosperity of the area has declined.

We do not know if there was ever a nucleated village on this site. Two houses near to the church stand on a very early track that runs down to Alfriston, and may be the sole occupants of the original village site. No early maps of the area survive, and only scanty documentary evidence as to population size exists.

In 1296 there were 21 taxpayers in the village, and it may be that following the Black Death of 1349 the community abandoned their hillside position and moved down to better watered sites at the base of the hill as a non-nucleated settlement. Certainly communities of this size were badly affected by plagues and found it possible to uproot themselves — unlike the larger villages where many other factors worked against abandonment of traditional sites.

THE MARDENS
NGR TQ796142

The Mardens are a group of four settlements on unspoilt downland that take their collective name from the Old English for boundary and hill. From the size and architecture of the three surviving churches it seems unlikely that any of the settlements was ever very wealthy. North Marden, now represented by just church and farm, gives the earliest architectural evidence – a twelfth century apsed structure. The churches at Up Marden and East Marden both date from the thirteenth century, whilst that at West Marden was demolished in the sixteenth century.

To the north and west of the church at North Marden are the humps and bumps typical of former house platforms, and pot sherds and slates found here have been dated to the twelfth and fourteenth centuries.

Domesday Book records the four manors separately – with a total population of about 50. Surprisingly the manor with the smallest recorded population did not have the smallest amount of land. This suggests that in later periods, following amalgamation of landholdings, overspill from one manor could be taken up by another and lead to larger communities. Today East Marden is the only one of the four to have a nucleated settlement.

There can be few such clear examples of a moving population within a well defined area – the moves being brought about by the change from cereal growing to sheep production and the subsequent loss in real value incomes.

MUNTHAM

NGR TQ105103

Muntham lies between Findon and Washington to the north of Worthing. Today represented by a farm, there are signs in the area that a small,
mobile community once existed. To the east of the A27 are a series of
medieval field systems (see plate section), whilst the supposed location
of the village of Muntham is on the opposite side of the valley. 'Ham' is
a common Old English place-name which indicates a homestead, usually
associated with farming, and is often prefixed, as in this case, by a
personal name.

In the Domesday Survey Muntham has no hides, but land for two
ploughs. There were 5 villagers and 6 smallholders. This area was part of
the manor of Findon – possibly grazing lands joined to the main settlement by a road running north up the valley. Excavations carried out in
the area through the 1950s showed signs of large scale Iron Age settlements and Roman pottery. This proves that for the early agricultural
settlers it was an ideal area, but that when the time came for settlements
to be accessible and near sources of finance and ready markets, those
that were in the remoter areas had to be abandoned.

NEWTIMBER

NGR TQ271133

Saddlescombe, which lies high on the Downs to the south of the present village of Newtimber, may have been the site of the original settlement – the Manor House and cottages sited around a small green. There was some arable land there – most of the parish being suitable for grazing only. Today there are still signs of medieval lynchets on Newtimber Hill, suggesting that arable farming on the hillside developed as far as it could.

At some stage a move must have been made into the flatter, more sheltered valley to the north, where a church was built at the centre of a nucleated settlement. This is probably when the place received its name, for it can easily be translated into 'the newly timbered building'.

Domesday records a mill in the parish, which must have stood in the valley, and which probably encouraged the new settlement to establish itself where it did. At first the manor was held by the Knights Templar, then the Hospitallers. In 1395 a record of Lewes Priory mentions 'the site of the manor', suggesting a move at about that time. For much of its history the manor was held by the de Cheyney family – who also held Hamsey.

In the seventeenth century the Great Plague of 1665, followed by the emparkation of Newtimber Place in about 1675 probably both contributed to a move from a nucleated settlement to a scattered community. This left the thirteenth century church isolated in a field, unaccompanied even by the late sixteenth century moated manor house.

NORTHEYE

NGR TQ683072

One of the charters which refer to the Drainage of the Hooe marshes refers to the Mereflete, a natural tidal creek which acted as the main drainage channel for the numerous artificial cuts ordered by the monks of Battle Abbey in the twelfth and thirteenth centuries.

The Abbey was involved in the reclamation of marsh to add fertile alluvial fields to their manor of Barnhorne. At the northern end of the Mereflete stood the small town of Northeye, which ultimately formed a limb of the Cinque Ports Confederation attached to Hastings. This would have been built on the eye, or island, that was probably the first reclaimed land to be suitable for habitation.

Today a number of footpaths converge at this windswept site, where a track from Barnhorne ends abruptly at the Mereflete channel. The depopulation of this site was almost certainly due to the silting up of the channel brought about by the coastal storms of the late fourteenth century. The chapel of St James, first mentioned in 1262, was recorded in a Parliamentary Survey of 1649, and its ruins survived until the 1850s, although there is nothing to be seen in the locality today.

OLD ERRINGHAM

NGR TQ205067

Several archaeological excavations in recent years have shown this side of the Adur valley to have been in continuous occupation for in excess of a thousand years. Regrettably mineral extraction has destroyed much evidence, and created a landscape which is more man-made than natural.

In 1964 a Saxon weaver's hut was discovered – indicating a small domestic community on these slopes, possibly belonging to Erra whose enclosed homestead, or tun, gave this place its name. At the time of Domesday there were about 60 acres of land supporting 2 villagers and 5 smallholders, 'who have nothing'. Whilst Erringham was never a parish in its own right, and always formed part of Shoreham, its manor had a chapel of ease – parts of which remain as a farm building. From detailed examination the remains are of 12th century date, and probably formed the chancel of a much larger building.

Whilst there are few documentary sources for Erringham and its decline, we can be sure that it was wealthy enough to support the chapel in the 13th century, and therefore probably declined as a result of the Black Death and subsequent changes in agricultural practice. It may also have been that the river – which formerly supported the manors of Annington (see Botolphs) and Coombes on the opposite side of the valley declined in importance. That it was used for the movement of building materials is known by the fact that slates found at Old Erringham have been identified as coming from quarries in South Devon.

As the estuary moved and its configuration changed, so the advantage of having the river at the base of Erringham Hill became less important. In addition, the lack of a wide valley floor on the east side of the river meant that cereal cultivation was not viable, and this alternative form of income could not be tapped.

ALCISTON. At the centre of the medieval village are the remains of the dovecote first mentioned in the 14th century.

ALDRINGTON. A late eighteenth century watercolour in the British Library of the church after it had been a ruin for nearly 200 years.

ARLINGTON. The parish church from the west, showing the earthworks known locally as 'the sluices'.

BALMER. An aerial view from the north. The medieval settlement appears to have been on the ridge to either side of the road at the bottom of this view.

Above: BALSDEAN VALLEY from the north. The flatter floor of the valley in the centre of this picture would have been the site of the medieval village, at the junction of the downland tracks.

Opposite page top: BALSDEAN CHAPEL. An eighteenth century watercolour in the British Library showing the Norman church demolished during the Second World War. This was the last surviving medieval building here.

Opposite page bottom: BARNHORNE. Looking from the horn of higher land to the marshes reclaimed in the thirteenth century and the Mereflete Channel.

BOTOLPHS. Aerial view showing the Saxon church in the centre. The field above the road shows clear earthworks of the former village of Annington.

BULVERHYTHE. The only medieval remains are the ruins of the former parish church, first mentioned in 1372.

BURPHAM. View of the Saxon Burgh from the south, showing its commanding position above the valley floor.

BUXTED. View of the church from the west, showing the ridge of house platforms on the left hand side.

COOMBES. The meadow to the east of the church that originally supported medieval houses.

EXCEAT. Aerial view to show the juxtaposition of the Cuckmere River (the loop bend in the bottom left hand corner) and downland (rising ground to the right). The area is now enforested.

FORD. The only medieval building to survive is the parish church which dates from the twelfth century.

HAMSEY. View from the west looking along the narrow promontory which was too narrow to allow medieval expansion.

HANGLETON. The parish church, the only reminder of a large and prosperous thirteenth century population.

LULLINGTON. The much visited church which comprises only the chancel of a larger thirteenth century building.

MUNTHAM. Excellent earthworks in the narrow valley to the north of Worthing show the track layout of this small settlement.

PARHAM. The best example in Sussex of a village being moved from its original grouping around the Medieval church.

RACTON. Racton church may just be seen in the centre of this view which shows the narrow valley floor.

TARRING NEVILLE. The protected field to the south of the church that would have been ideal for the medieval timber houses.

TELSCOMBE. The track which leads from the north side of the church down a protected valley towards the Ouse.

TIDE MILLS. The brick arches that supported the Mill. The town of Seaford is in the distance.

WARDOUR. The small group of houses on the edge of Pagham Harbour that probably stand on the site of the planned town of Wardour - which was to have been a new and reliable harbour for the city of Chichester.

WARMINGHURST. An estate map of 1707 which clearly shows the site of the former settlement 'Towne Feild' in the centre.

OLD SELSEY

NGR SZ871958

Whilst Selsey still exists as a major coastal settlement, it is included here for its historical importance, and for its medieval church which marks the position of the former town (see map on page 20).

This is one of the earliest recorded sites in Sussex, having been granted to St Wilfrid in AD681, when there was probably little more here than the seal-inhabited island from which the place name derives. It was here that he founded a monastery which in turn became a cathedral, and which was eventually moved to Chichester in 1075 as a result of the Council of Windsor which stipulated that cathedrals should no longer stand in rural areas.

At the time of the Domesday Survey Selsey was assessed at 10 hides, with 16 smallholders, 11 villagers and 2 slaves. At this period it was probably still an island, stretching much further south than today. Where the cathedral stood is unclear, although it was probably situated on the sea's edge, like the church of similar date at Bradwell in Essex.

The church, or portion of church, which survives today represents the thirteenth century chancel of a much larger building. It lay close to what at that time was a busy natural harbour, and it seems more than likely that a sizeable group of buildings stood there also. A manor house has existed in the centre of the former island for several hundred years, so the harbour settlement was probably built for purely commercial purposes.

In the middle of the last century the old church was partially demolished and moved to the new village centre where it was rebuilt – indicating that after some centuries of inconvenience the locals decided that enough was enough and gladly gave up their long journeys to weekly worship.

It is now almost universally accepted that the earthworks near the old church, of which the chancel was left standing, are associated with sixteenth and seventeenth century coastal defences, and are nothing to do with the previous settlement in the area. The old church is now cared for by the Churches Conservation Trust, who also look after the church at Warminghurst (see separate entry).

PANGDEAN

NRG TQ294117

Today Pangdean only consists of a farm and medieval field system on the side of the downs to the south of Pyecombe. In the Domesday Survey there were 20 villeins and 8 borderers, whilst in the mid twelfth century a church is mentioned. Dean is a common Sussex suffix to indicate a valley, and in this case is prefixed by a personal name, possibly Pega, who was the first person to be associated with a settlement on this site.

The depopulation of Pangdean is harder to explain than some of the neighbouring communities. Whilst the fall in the value of wool in the late fourteenth century would no doubt have contributed to the decline, the strategic position of Pangdean in the narrow valley would have been to its commercial advantage. This may suggest that the original settlement was higher up the hillside, at or near NGR 300310 where the land is slightly flatter. This location lies between the two medieval field systems that can still be identified today. If we also take into account the origin of the neighbouring village name of Pyecombe — which means 'gnat infested valley' — we have yet another piece of evidence to support a higher, rather than lower, position for Pangdean.

Following the death of Thomas de Poynings in October 1339 an inquisition was held to determine how much his landholding at Pangdean was worth. The 'capital messuage' (manor house) was valued at 12s a year, there was a sheepcote worth 50s a year, 3 acres of park and several pastures with 50 customary tenants.

Two later deeds, now in the library at Althorp House, mention Pangdean. The earliest, of 1445, settled the manor on Sir Richard Poynings, whilst the second, dating from eight years later, records its sale by Henry Earl of Northumberland to Sir Edward Seymour, together with the other 'lost' villages of Chington and Perching.

PARHAM

NGR TQ059141

Parham is one of the finest country houses in Sussex. The present mansion dates from the last quarter of the sixteenth century and was built by Sir Thomas Palmer, who had been granted the manor of Parham following the Dissolution of the Monasteries. Before that date the land had formed part of the estates of Westminster Abbey, and at Domesday had contained over six hundred acres, divided into two equal portions; probably one settlement standing in the valley, the other — which supported a much smaller population — on the downs to the south. That it was a farming settlement from the start seems probable from the place-name which combines the 'ham', or unenclosed farming homestead, with the place where 'pear trees grow', although this does not imply that other forms of agriculture were not conducted here.

As the lower settlement grew a church was built near the Manor House and a nucleated settlement became well established.

Following the sixteenth century change in ownership a deer park was established around the house — this is first mentioned in 1628. At the end of the seventeenth century the park was probably enlarged to the south, taking in the area of the village, and during the fifty years or so that followed the villagers abandoned their traditional homes and moved to Rackham, a long-established settlement half a mile to the west.

This left the parish church isolated in the deer park where it may still be visited today (see plate section). With its new-found position the church took the form more of a private family chapel than a parish church and as such was rebuilt in the opening years of the nineteenth century, complete with squire's pew and a fireplace to warm him whilst at prayer.

PERCHING

NGR TQ243103

At the time of the Domesday Survey Perching was divided into three manors. Each supported a population of only about ten. Two manors — those with less land — had a mill each, whilst the largest had a slightly larger landholding and population.

From this we can deduce that the main settlement was on the downland where extensive field systems can be found to the north of Mile Oak. The '-ing', or Scandinavian element of this name tells us that we are fairly near the coast, whilst the prefix possibly emphasises the point that these were enclosed settlements.

The two smaller manors, with their watermills, must have been some distance to the north in the lee of the downs, in the area now known as Fulking. Even today the Ordnance Survey maps show Perching Manor Farm and Perching Sands Farm over two miles to the north of the original settlement. It is more than likely that the track linking them was a medieval droveway that also served the mills.

The lay subsidy return for 1327 shows a taxable population of fourteen. Five years later this had been reduced to eleven, and by 1621 only seven residents are recorded. This equates to the changes in agricultural practice rather than the Black Death as the main reason for shrinkage and ultimate abandonment of the original settlement.

A deed of 1453 at Althorp House records the passing of the Lordship of the Manor of Perching from Henry Earl of Northumberland to Sir Edward Seymour (see also Chington and Pangdean).

PYECOMBE

NGR TQ293126

We can well understand the reason for Pyecombe not being built in the valley floor, as the name derives from the Old English for 'gnat-infested valley'! As a consequence the village was established on a small knob of land around the present church, which itself shows evidence of twelfth century work. A track leads to the north of the church towards the Warenne – and to the east of Wolstenbury Hill Iron Age fort. This track runs for some of its route along an artificial terrace, although whether this was constructed for the road, or developed as a result of it, is not clear. It is probable that there was never a manor of Pyecombe, the settlement being placed, for tax purposes, with neighbouring Pangdean. After Pangdean's decline, Pyecombe was for long associated with the village of Poynings in the opposite direction.

During the early seventeenth century Pyecombe was particularly affected by plague. The Church Registers – which start in 1561 – record these almost annual pestilences, the most serious of which occurred in 1603. Almost immediately the survivors abandoned their village in favour of a new settlement half a mile to the west, where it survives on the A23 today. At the time of this move the main Brighton road did not exist – it was created in 1810 – so the change of location was definitely not for commercial benefit.

In the 1603 Religious Survey, undertaken immediately before the plague, 50 worshippers are recorded at Pyecombe church. By 1621, following the move west, only 4 residents were assessed as taxpayers. The population then slowly returned to its former level – the 1664 Hearth Tax Returns recorded 14 houses – and by 1676 there were 52 residents.

RACTON

NGR TQ780092

Racton stands to the south of the Mardens, on equally poor land. It is on the east side of a valley, along the bottom of which runs a long-established road following, as is often the case, a small river. The valley gives Racton its name as it refers to the 'tun', or enclosed homestead, within the 'rac' which is from the Old English 'hrace', meaning a pass or neck.

At the time of Domesday there were 5 hides of land with 8 villagers and 13 smallholders. For this part of rural Sussex this was a sizeable population.

Today the tiny twelfth century church (first mentioned in 1142) and a few cottages survive, although it is not certain that they mark the site of the original settlement, the early centre of population possibly standing higher up the valley (see plate section). In 1445, following depopulation, the parish was joined to that of Lordington, and in 1535 was jointly valued at £5 19s 1d.

The manor house of Racton survived until the middle of the last century, when it was demolished. Parts of the building were salvaged and re-used at Racton Park Farm. From at least the fourteenth century the manor was held by the Gunter family. Colonel George Gunter helped Charles II escape to France via Brighton following the Battle of Worcester, and local tradition asserts that the King stayed the night in a cottage next to the church, although this is not borne out by contemporary accounts. The simple church contains many references to the family. The stonework of the east window shows their coat-of-arms, whilst there are two fascinating monuments to them in the chancel.

SHOREHAM, OLD AND NEW

NGR TQ216052

Although not 'lost' in the true sense of the word, the town of Shoreham has moved as a result of the silting up of the Adur estuary, occasioned by a spit of shingle which started growing towards the end of the eleventh century. This spit has in more recent times been developed as the area now called Shoreham Beach. Interestingly, Shoreham does not derive its name from the shore, on which the early settlement would not have survived, but from the Old English word *'scora'*, meaning a 'steep hill'. This, when taken with the suffix '-ham' meaning a farming homestead, shows that the early history of this place was agricultural rather than commercial.

Old Shoreham Church, dedicated to St Nicholas, dates from Saxon times, with a blocked north doorway of tenth century date. It was granted by William of Braose to the French Abbey of Saumur in 1075. In Domesday Book there were over 75 people living in Shoreham, and although there were over 600 acres of land within the manor, most of these would have been employed in the port. There is no inconsistency in these figures, for this book contains details of many rural communities with as much land, but only capable of supporting a population of less than a dozen.

At about this time a new church was being built further to the south and east to serve a growing commercial development, along the shore opposite the shingle spit. The new town was being laid out on the traditional grid system, with narrow parallel streets running down to the quayside. Most of these have been lost to subsequent coastal erosion, but the church, one of the most magnificent of its period in the county, survives towards the north-east corner of the new settlement.

STANMER

NGR TQ337096

A survey of 1608 shows quite plainly the extent of the medieval settlement. There were then 32 families living there, with evidence of multiple occupation of some dwellings. It had obviously been a large and prosperous settlement throughout the medieval period as at the time of Domesday there were 49 villagers and 10 smallholders and over 2000 acres of land, settled near the 'stoney lake', or mere, from which the village derives its name.

During the first half of the seventeenth century the Michelborne family, who had just acquired the manor, gradually purchased the freehold cottages in the village. This was mainly achieved by the restriction of the amount of common land available. Without this essential grazing land the smallholder's existence was considerably threatened.

The location of the houses is still to be seen to the north-west of the church, in the form of an open field with mounds. The present village street opposite takes the form of a row of eighteenth and nineteenth century houses running along the valley floor.

To the north of the village lies the deserted settlement known locally as Piddingworth – where medieval field systems survive on a south facing downland slope. Two cottages there were occupied until the last war, and a few flint walls survive. The name may be linked to that of Pidda who gave his name to Piddinghoe, a few miles to the east at Newhaven, although no further records survive.

SUTTON

NGR TV494997

Sutton does not appear in the Domesday Survey, although from the tax returns of the early fourteenth century it seems to have been a fairly well-populated settlement, the greater portion of which was held by Michelham Priory. The name is straightforwardly interpreted as the 'southern town' and may have been one of a series of small settlements on the southern slopes of the Downs escarpment.

In 1327 eighteen householders are recorded, falling to eight five years later. The 1341 Inquisition gives poor weather as the cause, no doubt helped by French raiding parties. It had a church – the ruins of which survived well into the last century, but from 1509 the parish had been united to that of Seaford, indicating a small population.

At some stage before 1260 a small religious Hospital dedicated to St James was founded at Sutton, possibly by the Abbey of Robertsbridge who were the lords of the manor. By the 16th century it had evidently closed and its revenue had been united with that of the chapel at Barpham (see separate entry) to pay for a stall in Chichester Cathedral. In 1534 the site of the Hospital, known as Spittel-land, was let to John Seman together with ten acres of land.

Today the area is covered by modern housing, and now forms a suburb of Seaford.

TARRING NEVILLE

NGR TQ 444039

The suffix, Neville, was added in the thirteenth century when the manor was held by a family of that name. There was, however, an earlier Scandanavian settlement, indicated by the '-ing' in Tarring. In Domesday Book it was recorded as Toringes, with a population of 11 villagers, 9 smallholders and 3 slaves.

The village was gathered in a small combe on the eastern side of the Ouse valley, protected from the coastal winds. It is regarded locally as a good example of a village depopulated as a result of plague, but there is no documentary evidence to support this, and it seems more likely that its depopulation occurred as a result of the familiar thirteenth century agricultural changes.

The medieval parish was a very odd shape, following the Ouse for two miles in length and stretching up the slope of the downs for just a mile at its widest part. This relatively small area of very mixed agricultural land would not have been sufficient to support a large population. In the seventeenth century the parish was united to that of South Heighton (Denton), showing that a nadir had been reached.

Today only a church, dating from the thirteenth century, and a farm survive in the combe, although it is easy to conjure up a group of small cottages on the flat land to the south of the church (see plate section).

TELSCOMBE

NGR TQ 405033

It seems likely that there was a Saxon settlement, founded by a chief called Tittle, in a valley near the present church, although it is not mentioned under that name in the Domesday Survey. Horsfield, writing in 1835, suggested that because of its position in the Domesday Survey, and because the size of land is comparable, Telscombe is recorded under the name of Laneswice. In AD996 King Edgar granted the manor to the Abbey of Hyde who held it until the Reformation.

There are not many medieval records to help us quantify the size of population here, but there was obviously enough money available in the early twelfth century to build a small, but substantial, church which survives today (see plate section). Shortly afterwards a small tower was added, together with a north aisle. Our next firm evidence does not appear until the 18th century, when Burrell wrote:

'When I was there I found a large breach in the roof of the body of the church, the room and seats (which were almost destroyed) defiled with bird dun, and a Pigeon on the Communion Table. On enquiry I found that the Rector lived in London and that there was no Register kept according to the form prescribed by Act of Parliament and that the births, marriages and burials are entered promiscuously.'

Therefore, by the 18th century the population was so small and remote that they weren't bothered about maintaining their church. At about the same time it was recorded in another source that the population was entirely composed of smugglers – which wouldn't have helped the situation!

TIDE MILLS

It is not often that a 'lost village' is found to have been built and abandoned within the past three hundred years. The Tide Mills in question were built in the eighteenth century to take advantage of the silted-up end of the former Ouse estuary.

Throughout the Middle Ages the river entered the sea at Seaford – hence the name. On the slopes some miles to the west stood the early settlement of Meeching. After 1539 landowners in the Ouse valley, wishing to ease drainage problems, decided to straighten the river by cutting a new estuary nearer Meeching. This is one of the earliest

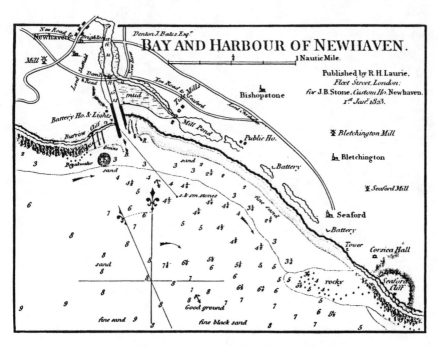

Tide Mills. Early nineteenth century map which clearly shows the coastline and the tidal pond created by the new outfall of the River Ouse.

canalisation projects in Britain. By opening up the thin spit of land near Meeching a new port was constructed – the New Haven – as it became known.

This left an arm of the Ouse stretching from Newhaven to Seaford as a tidal inlet. Following an Act of Parliament of 1761 a large tide mill was constructed to take advantage of this natural energy. It reached its peak fifty years later under the management of one William Catt. The mill was in operation sixteen hours a day, producing 1500 sacks of flour per week.

Houses for the sixty or so mill workers were constructed, and a railway halt built especially for their use. Today a few brick arches, flint walls and abandoned railway platforms are all that remain from this former industrial settlement, and the tide still flows into the much reduced inlet to the east (see plate section).

TWINEHAM

NGR TQ 253200

There is no mention of Twineham in the Domesday Survey, but it was probably entered as Benefelle, which survives as the name of a manor house in the parish today. At that time it had depreciated in value tremendously from 3 hides and 1 virgate to nothing. There was land for 9 villagers, and 8 smallholders, with meadows, and woodland for pigs. The current name of Twineham is entirely English in origin and means 'the homestead between the streams'.

The fact that three footpaths meet at the church points to the fact that a small settlement must have existed around the church when it was built in the sixteenth century. It is rare to find an isolated church being built on a new site at such a late date, so it must be the case of a nucleated community becoming spread out over a number of years.

The present church dates entirely from the sixteenth century and is one of the earliest churches to have been built of brick. However, it contains a thirteenth century font from the previous building, which was first recorded in 1226.

There are many ancient houses scattered across the parish, some of which have associations with the Knights Hospitaller, who held them as outlying parts of the manor of Saddlescombe.

UPPER BARPHAM

NGR TQ068089

The Subsidy Rolls of the late thirteenth and early fourteenth centuries suggest that even before the Black Death there was a decline in population at this isolated site, a site first mentioned in Domesday. This is important because it proves that the changes in agricultural practice that affected so many other places at about the time of the Black Death were just as much to blame for depopulation as the plague itself. Barpham takes its name from the old Celtic word for hill, 'barr', plus the 'ham' of an English homestead, the latter being especially used for farming settlements.

The rural population declined as people moved into towns in the hope of improving their standard of living. As a result, the remaining community was forced to abandon labour intensive cereal growing in favour of sheep husbandry, which required fewer people. This gradual change was hastened by the onset of the Black Death in 1349, but may already have been complete in tiny isolated settlements like Barpham.

The last rector was instituted here in 1521, by which time the population was probably minute. Disciplined excavation of the church foundations in 1952 revealed a complicated building, much damaged by nineteenth century treasure seekers. It showed a not insubstantial church displaying signs of six separate building periods spanning about 400 years, ending in the fourteenth century. This is a sure sign of the loss of prosperity occasioned by depopulation at this crucial time in English history. Several shallow children's graves of probably fourteenth century date tended to confirm the impact of the plague here.

WARDOUR (SIDLESHAM)

NGR TQ860970

We have no record of who the Saxon Sidel was, but he was of some importance as the manor has carried his name since at least AD683 when it was mentioned in a charter. In 1262 Bishop Stephen of Chichester attempted to establish a new town within the boundaries of his manor of Sidlesham (see map on page 20). This was probably to provide Chichester with a reliable Harbour — the villages that existed on what is now the Chichester Channel were already suffering from coastal problems.

To encourage settlers in the new port the Bishop granted many financial privileges, the principal one being the right to sell, without charge, at any other fair or market that he owned. However, it seems that the new town was not a success and failed soon after its foundation.

Today there is no trace of settlement, but as it was designed as a port it must have been in the southern part of the manor of Sidlesham (see plate section), either near the Ferry House on the main Selsey Road, or slightly further east where the Crab and Lobster Inn occupies a quayside setting today, surrounded by picturesque eighteenth century houses.

WARMINGHURST

NGR TQ117169

Today there is little to be seen at Warminghurst apart from the thirteenth century church splendidly maintained by the Churches Conservation Trust. It has no village centre, and a very small population. The land
is still well-wooded with hazel and ash and the types of tree so often
associated with the suffix '-hurst', meaning light, often coppiced, woodland. The first part of the name refers to an individual, possibly a Saxon
called Wyrm. In documentary evidence before the thirteenth century the
place is always suffixed by 'tun' meaning an enclosed homestead, and it
is a mystery why 'hurst' had been substituted by 1296 when it appears
as such in the lay subsidy roll.

Warminghurst was originally part of the manor of Steyning given by
Edward the Confessor to the Abbey of Fecamp in Normandy. The
Abbey sent a bailiff to manage the entire estate, and by local tradition he
lived at Warminghurst, in a grange with chapel attached. In 1414 the
resident steward was ordered to send 100 oaks from these lands to help
the Earl of Arundel in his attempts to protect Calais from French attack.
As Warminghurst was so isolated from Fecamp, the stewards were open
to corruption and some were convicted of selling wood for their own
personal gain.

In the British Library is an Estate Map of 1707 which shows the area
around the church (see plate section). The major building on the map is
Warminghurst Place – the park of which was first mentioned in 1345,
and which would have precluded the existence of houses to the south
and west of the church. The map is of interest in that it names each field,
and just to the north and east of the church is a 6 acre field called
'Towne' field – indicating the tradition that the former village was lo-
cated in this position.

WEST BLATCHINGTON

NGR TQ278065

The church of St Peter, West Blatchington, which mainly dates from the mid 20th century contains, as its south aisle, the substantial remains of a late Saxon single-cell church. These rectangular buildings were indicative of the simple constructions erected by villagers for their own use before the days of organised builders. This served the manor of Blatchington for over five hundred years until, following enclosure in the early sixteenth century, the population declined and the church fell out of use.

The history of Blatchington parallels that of the neighbouring parish of Hangleton. Indeed, until the Norman conquest Blatchington was a chapelry within the parish of Hangleton. It takes its name from the 'tun' or enclosure round the homestead – of a tribe ruled by the chieftain Blaecca.

The pre-Conquest boundary of the Blatchington estate was formed by earthworks – which still survive in part to the east of the parish. This estate was then split into two separate manors, each based on a single existing church. The main problem with this assumption is that Blatchington (whose church displays unquestionable pre-Conquest architecture) does not appear in the Domesday Survey – in an area which is otherwise fairly accurately documented. Writing in the Sussex Archaeological Collections in 1988 John Holmes suggested that the church mentioned under the entry for Patcham is actually Blatchington Church, as the manors of Blatchington and Patcham had been amalgamated by William de Warenne and the church for Patcham had yet to be built. Later the two manors were split, and Blatchington became a separate entity.

By the seventeenth century the only family to use Blatchington church was that of Scrase, the lords of the manor. They had enclosed the open field system and created what in effect was a self sufficient estate for themselves and their servants. In the mid 1650s the family became attached to the Society of Friends, and this resulted in the parish church being abandoned completely until its rescue from almost complete destruction in 1890, and its resultant restoration and subsequent enlargement to cope with the growth of Hove.

WEST TARRING

The village is first mentioned in a charter of AD940, and is – by its name – of Scandinavian origin but the first accurate description of the settlement occurs in the Domesday Book when the manor was divided into two parts. The larger, representing 7 hides and 1 virgate, was held by the Archbishop of Canterbury. There were 27 villagers, 14 smallholders and 2 churches. The smaller, of 4 hides and held by William de Braose, supported just 4 villagers and 5 smallholders.

The importance of the village lay in the fact that it was not just another holding of the Archbishop, but that it actually had an ecclesiastical palace. Part of this building survives in use as a public hall, and dates from the thirteenth century, as does the parish church.

Excavations carried out in 1964 established that there was no evidence of earlier occupation in the village. This is surprising in view of its documented history, and points to the fact that it probably moved within its manorial boundaries at some point in its first three hundred year recorded history. As an outer suburb of modern Worthing it is not easy to locate any earlier site for the settlement, but whilst nearby Durrington is mentioned in Domesday Book, the adjacent Salvington is not, and may represent the former site of Tarring.

WINCHELSEA

NGR TQ 905175

Severe storms in the middle of the thirteenth century lead to the abandonment of the old port of Winchelsea which stood on the levels somewhere in the region of present day Camber Sands. It must have been situated on a bend in the River Brede as the place-name comes from the Old English *'wincel'*, or 'corner', and 'eye', which means island.

The earliest recorded storms – in October 1250 – brought high tides that submerged part of the town, whilst the second and more devastating storm of October 1287 caused the River Rother to divert its course. Until that time it had flowed north of the İsle of Oxney to an estuary at New Romney in Kent, but the storm threw up a shingle bank there, and the river found a new course south of Oxney to meet the sea at Winchelsea, washing most of it away in the process.

Edward I had already started to lay out a replacement town. In 1280 he had acquired the manor of Iham on a hilltop position three miles to the north-west. In September 1292 the burgage plots were finally handed over by the Bishop of Ely acting on behalf of the King, who in turn gave them a helping hand in the establishment of the new town by allowing its residents the first seven years rent free. Much has been written about the new Winchelsea, and it seems likely that it was never fully occupied, and that the King went back on his promise by charging full rents almost from the start.

The town was planned on a large scale – with over 40 houses in the north-east corner having vaulted cellars to house barrels of wine imported from Gascony - the trade on which the new town was to depend for its prosperity. There were originally three churches, the largest of which, St Thomas's, was allotted a whole block on the street grid. Of the three it is the only one to survive, athough just the chancel and ruinous transepts remain of the original 14th century building.

After such a well-planned start the later history of Winchelsea is one of steady decline. The River Brede, which linked the town to the coast started to silt up, creating very difficult harbour access. To compound their problems the townsfolk suffered four raids by the French, during which a large part of St Thomas Church was destroyed. By the sixteenth century there were less than 60 inhabited houses, and today less than a third of the original burgage plots may be seen.

WISTON

NGR TQ155124

Wiston Park house was built by Sir Thomas Shirley in 1575, and any village that still existed would have been obliterated by his emparkations. However it seems that the village had all but disappeared anyway, At Domesday there were 10 villagers, 24 smallholders and 5 slaves, whose landholdings were recorded as being worth 'nothing'. The 'tun' or enclosed settlement that had originally belonged to Wigstan no longer provided a viable income.

In 1345 18 tenants were recorded, with one plot untenanted, but in 1356 following the Black Death of 1349, 8 plots of land were untenanted, showing the affect of the plague in this part of the county.

The church, which was much restored in the nineteenth century, dates from the period just before the Black Death – and the lack of any later work proves that the population was either too small or too poor to undertake any more work.

Its position on a ridge to the north of the downs would have been well-drained, but very exposed. The neighbouring settlement of Buncton, which had a centrally placed church serving a small non-nucleated community, shows an almost identical pattern of development.

WOODMANCOTE

NGR TQ231151

A small agricultural community existed here at the time of the Domesday Survey, totalling 20 householders, some of whom must have worked in forestry as the place-name is derived from the Old English for woodman's cottages. Nothing survives from the medieval period, except tiny parts of the church. No doubt the fairly flat ground near the church would have been the site of the village, but this now forms part of the park of Woodmancote Place, and there do not appear to be any surviving earthworks. All the other houses in the immediate area today are of later periods.

One of the few surviving medieval documents to mention the village is a manuscript of Richard II absolving a group of men of an excommunication placed on them some time earlier. As part of their penance they had to give half a pound of wax candle to the church at Woodmancote – showing that at least one of them must have lived there.